CAREER ANCHORS

THE CHANGING NATURE OF WORK AND CAREERS

FACILITATOR'S GUIDE

FOURTH EDITION

Edgar H. Schein
John Van Maanen

WILEY

Published by Wiley
One Montgomery Street, Suite 1200, San Francisco, CA 94104-4594
www.wiley.com

ISBN: 978-1-118-45574-6

Acquiring Editor: Holly Allen
Director of Development: Kathleen Dolan Davies
Production Editor: Dawn Kilgore
Editor: Rebecca Taff
Manufacturing Supervisor: Becky Morgan

Printing 10 9 8 7 6 5 4 3 2 1

Contents

Introduction

THE MAIN PURPOSE OF THIS GUIDE is to familiarize the coach or facilitator with what is in the two accompanying booklets: the *Career Anchors Self-Assessment* (survey) and the *Career Anchors Participant Workbook* (interview and exercises). Before you attempt to use the Self-Assessment and Workbook with others, you should take the time to review and familiarize yourself with both pieces.

The concept of career anchors grew out of longitudinal research on men and women in different occupations. The primary application of this concept is in career counseling and coaching to help adults in early, mid, and late career identify what they really value in a job or career and what they would not give up if forced to make a choice.

The survey is a forty-item questionnaire intended to help the person who takes it identify his or her values. The scoring key gives the person a profile of his or her commitment to the various anchor categories. The anchor categories are described briefly. For some purposes, this will be sufficient to help the individual begin thinking about career development issues. The survey can, therefore, be used by itself. However, for many participants, the survey is just a warm-up that raises questions and opens up possibilities, but does not really resolve the issue of what their career anchors are and what they should do to align their anchors with their career development and other family/life issues.

The Participant Workbook (1) provides a more complete picture of career development; (2) makes the important distinction between the "internal" career and the externally defined stages in most occupations; (3) provides an interview guide to examine the participant's career history; (4) contains a more complete description of each of the anchor categories; (5) introduces the concept of job analysis through role mapping; (6) provides a way to help the participant sort out work career and family/life responsibilities; (7) describes some of the changes that are occurring in the world of work; and (8) provides a self-rating questionnaire to help the respondent identify developmental needs for further career growth and development.

In this edition we have made *three important changes*: (1) we enhanced the section on career development; (2) we have added an important exercise to help participants to analyze work career and family/life responsibilities; and (3) we greatly enhanced the text on what is happening in the world of work and discussed the implications for different career anchors. In order to do any kind of realistic career and family/life planning for the future, the participants will need to know how much things have changed, so we provided both research findings and our own speculations.

The interview is important because it provides a better and more complete picture of what the individual values, what motivates him or her, and what his or her self-perceived competencies are. But knowing oneself without knowing enough about a job or career is pointless. Therefore, good career planning, both from the point of view of the incumbent and from the point of view of the manager trying to fill a job, also requires a process for analyzing the essential characteristics of a job or career.

For this purpose, the second half of the workbook provides a process for analyzing the job the participant currently holds through role mapping that helps him or her to figure out who the main stakeholders of the job are, what their expectations are, and how that fits with his or her career anchor. It also provides a priority grid on which the participant can locate his or her current and desired "family/life situation" in terms of nine adaptive categories, each of which is a workable arrangement but presents different kinds of problems to be resolved.

For those situations in which the participant is looking for personal growth of skills, there is a concluding section in the workbook on career development. This section provides a self-assessment tool that allows the participant to rate him- or herself on the main analytical, interpersonal, and emotional dimensions that he or she may need to fulfill in some future job. The workbook ends with the invitation for the participant to make a developmental plan with concrete steps and timetables.

Especially in times of transition such as we are experiencing in today's rapidly evolving global economy, people must find out what their career anchors are in order to make intelligent plans for the future—to decide what industry to pursue, what job level to seek or settle for, what sort of work life they wish to live, what functional and interpersonal skills to highlight in the search for the next job, and how to assess their career potential with various employers. In more stable times, we could remain unaware of our career anchors, but if more choices have to be made, it becomes more important to know what one's inner priorities are, that is, what one would not want to give up.

This Facilitator's Guide provides various options for you as career coach and/ or manager to provide help to people as they attempt to improve the way they manage their own careers. This guide begins by describing how the *Career Anchors Self-Assessment* and *Career Anchors Participant Workbook* can be used, providing several options, and also includes a section specifically for managers who will be using the materials for themselves and/or with their direct reports. The next section provides some background information on why role mapping is particularly helpful for managers and managerial groups doing succession planning. Following this is a section on workshop designs, offering half-day and two-hour options. Finally, some recommendations for development planning and career implications are offered. This guide closes with a list of references and additional reading; this information is also provided to participants in the workbook.

How to Use the *Career Anchors Self-Assessment* Survey

THE CAREER ANCHORS SELF-ASSESSMENT survey is NOT a standardized test to be used to classify people. It is an aid to self-insight. It should NOT be used by you or by managers or coaches as a diagnostic tool, but rather as an aid to self-diagnosis and coaching.

There are two basic options for using the survey:

1. *Utilize the* Career Anchors Self-Assessment *on its own.* If time is short and/or a large number of participants are being introduced to the career anchor concept, it may be sufficient to just use the self-assessment and answer participants' questions after they have scored themselves. But in that case you should emphasize the importance of honesty; if participants are not totally honest with themselves when completing the assessment, they can easily have a biased view of what their values really are. The self-assessment is thus a good *introduction* to the concepts. But to gain full value out of the exercise, the facilitator should strongly recommend going on with the participant workbook and the interview instructions shown in the workbook.
2. *Utilize both the self-assessment and the participant workbook.* The *Career Anchors Self-Assessment* and the *Career Anchors Participant Workbook* are designed to be self-administering. If a participant buys the materials directly from the publisher, he or she should be able to go through the various exercises alone. The workbook recommends finding a partner with whom to do a mutual career interview, but many participants find this too time-consuming and just settle for what they can accomplish by themselves. In any case, you can recommend to participants that if they just want to go ahead on their own, it is perfectly feasible to do that by finding their own interview partners. Ideally, a partner should be a person who knows the participant well and is familiar with his or her career history. Often this is a spouse or close friend. We also think it helpful for the participant to also interview the partner as something of a return favor and as a way to further explore the participant's own anchor by contrast with another.

How to Use the Participant Workbook

IN THE FACILITATOR ROLE, you have several options for the use of the Career Anchors materials.

Option 1: Individual Career Counseling or Coaching

The *Career Anchors Participant Workbook* is a good way to start a career coaching session. If you are working with an individual, start with the survey and then do the career history interview from the *Career Anchors Participant Workbook.* Another option is to start with the interview before you reveal the anchor categories. Once people see the categories, they have a strong urge to locate themselves, which prematurely biases the coaching session. It is sometimes better for you to have the history as context to help the person gain self-insight. In that instance, you would use the survey after the interview and then look at anchor categories based on all of the information you now have.

The goal of the Participant Workbook is to increase self-insight. The anchor categories facilitate this, but it is not necessary for a person to clearly fit one category. If you are satisfied that the person now has a good picture of himself or herself, even though it cuts across anchors, that is a sufficient outcome. Sometimes people feel that several of the categories fit them equally well, and it is your role as a coach to judge whether or not they have done sufficient self-analysis.

What to Do If No Clear Anchor Shows Up

There are several possible reasons why a person might not come out with a clear anchor, and each requires a different approach to help the participant gain more self-insight. If there are some high scores around several anchors, then it is most helpful to get the person to zero in on what he or she would not give up if forced to make a choice. The best way to do this is to invent questions couched in future terms that would force a choice between the anchor categories.

Example: The person says that he wants to remain in his technical area of engineering and also wants to climb on the general management ladder. He insists that he has both a technical/functional and managerial anchor. You could ask him whether in some ideal future he would rather be the chief engineer of a big corporation or the executive vice president of that corporation. Most people will quickly choose one or the other, which reveals what they care about more deeply—the technical area or general management.

Another approach is to ask whether one of the categories is a "concern right now," but not really a career anchor.

Example: The person says that she is equally anchored in security and entrepreneurial creativity. Ask whether the security concern is really an anchor or a necessary concern at this stage of her career because of family or other personal issues. Point out that there are times in life when security is paramount, but that does not make it an anchor, only a here-and-now "concern."

Sometimes the individual cannot relate to any of the categories or says that three or four of them fit. One possibility is that the person has not had enough life experience to have formed a coherent self-image (anchor). In that case, encourage a variety of experiences to help the individual gather more real-life data about him- or herself. Sometimes the individual has had life experiences that do not resolve neatly into one of the anchor categories. The purpose of the exercise is to gain self-insight, not to stereotype oneself, so you should be supportive of the person finding his or her own vocabulary or concepts to describe him- or herself. There is no a priori value in forcing the person into a category.

Sometimes the anchor category is bell clear to you, the interviewer or coach, based on the career history, but you sense that the person is unable or unwilling to see what may be obvious to you. In that case, you should gently review with the person the career events and the reasons given for them with the added prompt of "What conclusion do you draw from what you have said?"

If the survey has been used, ask the participant which items he or she most strongly agreed with or disagreed with, and together examine each of those items in terms of "Why did you choose that one?"

In any event, the most important point to emphasize for the participant is that "This is not a test; the purpose is not to put you into a category; the purpose is to help you figure yourself out—to gain some insight into what you care about and what you think your own strengths and weaknesses are with respect to your career."

Option 2: Use the Self-Assessment and the Workbook in a Group Setting

Hand out both the self-assessment and workbook with instructions for participants to pair up and do their own interviews. This option works best in a classroom setting where both the self-assessment and workbook can be given out in one session. Have the participants complete both the self-assessment and career history interviews (in whatever order you feel works for the group). After the interviews you may want to bring the group together for a question-and-answer session on career anchors generally and for the participants to share their reactions to and insights gained through the self-diagnosis process.

Ideally, you would distribute both the self-assessment and the workbook a week or two in advance with instructions for the participants to bring back their results to a group session that could involve from four to fifty people. In setting up the group session, you can clarify the anchor categories and answer any questions that the participants may have regarding the career anchor concepts.

Then form small groups of five or six participants and ask each person to share his or her career anchor and reasoning with the others in his or her group. If the group is composed of people who know one another (from work, from school, from a program, etc.), it may be useful to ask those in the small groups to first guess the career anchors of the others in that group. This provides useful feedback to participants (in terms of how they are "seen" by others) as well as illustrating to those in the group that we typically aren't good judges of what really interests and drives each of us—that the career anchor is an "internal" not an "external" concept.

You might then lead a final general session asking the groups to share their reactions to the small group exchange and collect data from the group as to which anchors are most or least common, leading to a discussion of what is happening in the world of work that the participants should be conscious of.

This way of using the self-assessment and workbook has worked especially well in executive development programs, where the potential conflict among, for example, the technical/functional anchor, the general management anchor, the autonomy anchor, and the lifestyle anchor becomes most visible. If participants bring up the issue of having no clear anchor, apply the same suggested resolutions as were mentioned above for the individual counseling. Sometimes participants wonder what the "proper" or "average" distribution of anchors might or should be in, say, their respective professions or organizations or society. The answer, of course, is that there isn't one—distributions will vary by time, by group, by country, and for a thousand other reasons. The tried but true answer here is "it all depends."

While there are no norms or standard distributions associated with career anchors, participants often do appreciate learning how some other group or groups compare to their own. But, again, it is imperative that you point out that career anchor distributions vary considerably from group to group, organization to organization, occupation to occupation, even society to society. All distributions are sensitive to variations in educational backgrounds, age, workplace policies, economic conditions, and cultural (and sub-cultural) values of the individuals who make up the group. The Looking Ahead portion of the workbook highlights some of the broader social and organizational factors that may influence career anchor distributions.

Table 1. Career Anchors: MIT-Sloan Fellows Program (1996–2012)

General Management	33%
Lifestyle	12%
Entrepreneurial	12%
Challenge	11%
Service	9%
Technical/Functional	8%
Autonomy	8%
Security/Stability	4%
Unable to decide	3%

N = 1,171

Table 2. Career Anchors: MIT Sloan Fellows Program (2011)

General Management	22%
Entrepreneurial	15%
Challenge	14%
Lifestyle	13%
Service	11%
Technical/Functional	10%
Autonomy	8%
Security/Stability	4%
Unable to decide	3%

N = 101

Table 3. Career Anchors: MIT Sloan Fellows Program (1996)

General Management	37%
Challenge	15%
Lifestyle	11%
Entrepreneurial	9%
Service	8%
Technical/Functional	8%
Autonomy	6%
Security/Stability	3%
Unable to decide	3%

N = 49

With these important qualifiers in mind, an anchor distribution example is given below. The data are drawn from the Sloan Fellows in Innovation and Global Leadership program at MIT. This is an intensive, mid-career, one-year residential MBA program in the Sloan School of Management. The overall distribution of career anchors across a sixteen-year time span is presented first (Table 1), followed by the distributions for two cadres in the program, one recent (2011) (Table 2) and one not so recent (1996) (Table 3). The more recent class size reflects the growth of the program over the sixteen-year period. As you can see, the distributions vary—although not dramatically so—but several features stand out.

Across all classes, as might be expected given the characteristics of those who apply and are selected into the program, general management is the largest category—20 to 40 percent of a given class. This is to be expected, for Sloan is not, after all, a cooking school. The remaining seven anchors are all represented, although from year to year the numbers shift. There are always members of the class who cannot or will not designate a single anchor, but they are few in number. Our experience in using career anchors tells us that typically about 80 percent of any given group are comfortable selecting a single guiding anchor, even though they sometimes struggle to arrive at such a choice.

In looking at these distributions, keep in mind that this program is a highly selective one. It is designed for managers and professionals who are between the ages of thirty-five and forty-five and have ten to twenty years of work experience. About 65 to 75 percent of each class comes from the private sector, and well over half are technically trained in engineering, in the physical or natural sciences, in medicine, in law, etc.

The number of women in each class over the years varies by class from 15 to 30 percent—increasing of late. The program is also an international one with from 50 to 60 percent of the members of each cadre coming from outside the United States—from Latin America, Asia, Africa, the Middle East, and Europe, with a smattering of members from other parts of the world such as New Zealand, Australia, the Caribbean Islands, and so on. In other words, this is hardly a "representative group" of either professionals or managers, but then, it is difficult if not impossible to imagine what kind of group would be "representative" of such broad and diverse occupational worlds. Some of the articles in the References and Additional Reading section describe anchor distributions in other occupations.

Option 3. Use the Role Map to Analyze a Selected Job

The participant workbook includes a section that invites the participant to draw a role map of his or her present job. How to do that is fully described in the workbook. The construction of role maps for selected jobs that are of interest to the participant(s), and the analysis of stakeholders can be done as a separate exercise with or without having done the career anchor analysis. The important part of this activity is the role map, which makes the participant aware of the complexity of his or her job, the multiple demands that any job creates, and the connections between what role senders demand and what the participant as job holder can provide.

If future jobs are to be mapped and analyzed, there must be two or more participants who know something about those jobs. However, drawing an "imagined" role map for a possible future job can also be useful as a set of hypotheses to then be checked with someone in that job.

Working with Role Maps

It is important to help participants understand that jobs are more than what is in the job description, that jobs are embedded in role networks, and that as the world becomes more linked into networks of various kinds, the nature of work and work relationships will change in unpredictable ways. So everyone should have available the role mapping tool to analyze the current job he or she is in and possible future jobs he or she might consider.

You should help participants in the various workshop contexts or in individual counseling to draw the role maps and go over the concepts of role ambiguity, overload, and conflict described below. In the workshop context, it is probably useful as well to have the participants discuss in groups how they cope with each of these role issues to encourage participants to learn from each other.

Role Ambiguity, Role Overload, and Role Conflict

Role ambiguity occurs if you have key role senders, but you are not clear what it is that they actually expect of you. If you are experiencing "role ambiguity" with respect to selected stakeholders, you have basically two choices: (1) you can develop a communication process to reduce the ambiguity (that is, go to the stakeholders and ask them to share their expectations or give them your perceptions and ask them to modify them) or (2) you may decide to "live with the ambiguity" (that is, watch carefully how their future behavior provides clues until you have deciphered what they want). Obviously, alternative 1 is the better way to cope if you have access and opportunity to obtain "role clarification." But you have to take the initiative because the stakeholder may not be aware that he or she is sending ambiguous signals.

Role overload occurs when you realize that the sum total of what your critical stakeholders expect of you far exceeds what you are able to do. If the stakeholders are not equally important to you, role overload is typically handled by ignoring the expectations of the less important stakeholders, but this manner of coping often creates difficulties because the ignored stakeholders may react powerfully to being ignored.

A second coping mechanism for overload is to compromise on each stakeholder's expectations by doing only a part of what each of them expects. Unfortunately, this may make you look relatively less competent in their eyes. The reality that you are truly "too busy" may not be convincing to them if they do not know what your role map looks alike.

The best way of coping with overload is to communicate the situation to your key stakeholders and involve them in the process of setting priorities so that you do not have to guess what is important to others. The stakeholders may not even be aware of each other's expectations. Once you communicate to them that they have overloaded you, they can decide among themselves what is most important, or they can choose to empower you to make the decision.

Role conflict occurs when you realize that two or more stakeholders expect things of you that are in conflict with each other. This occurs most often in one of three forms: (1) what your superiors want is opposite to what your subordinates want, (2) what one of your peer stakeholders wants is in conflict with what another peer wants, or (3) what one of your critical stakeholders wants is in conflict with your expectations of yourself. Each of us is a stakeholder in our own job/role, and as such we have expectations of ourselves. Often we find that we are unwilling for any of a number of reasons to do what is expected of us, leading to ethical, moral, and motivational dilemmas.

In each of these instances, role renegotiation with the stakeholders is essential so that the emotional cost of conflict can be minimized. What this means in practice is that you must find a way to communicate to the various stakeholders how their expectations create conflict so that they can become involved in the resolution or else decide to empower you to resolve the conflict. If you act unilaterally to resolve the conflict, you run the risk of disappointing some stakeholder and giving the impression either that you are not motivated or not competent to meet his or her expectations.

A special case of overload or conflict occurs when the expectations of your family or friends conflict with the expectations of your work stakeholders. This type of "work/family overload and/or conflict" is becoming more prevalent and will become an ever bigger problem as organizational boundaries loosen. For example, overload may be reduced if more work is done at home. But work at home may involve assumptions about responsibility and commitment that are out of line with current assumptions about organization/employee relationships. To solve this kind of problem requires not only an understanding of the future form of organizations, but may involve complex negotiations with both the work organization and the family, and ultimately some change in cultural assumptions about the nature of work. Participants with the lifestyle anchor are particularly vulnerable in this area and need the reassurance that their situations are neither unique nor unsolvable.

Option 4: Use the Work Career and Family/Life Priority Grid in a Group Setting

The Work Career and Family/Life Priority Grid section of the participant workbook asks participants to assess just how they currently allocate their work, family, and other personal responsibilities and commitments. This can be done as a separate exercise with or without having completed the career anchor analysis. To fill out the grid requires the participant to also judge his or her partner's current priorities. When both have been determined, participants can locate themselves in one of nine cells on the grid. Each cell represents a distinct work career/family/life pattern that carries particular challenges. And each pattern is more or less difficult to manage given a particular career anchor. If possible, participants should have conversations with their respective partners and together figure out where they currently fit on the grid. How the grid is used and what the various cells mean is described in the workbook.

If participants do not have a partner (are single, divorced, or separated), ask that they consider past partners, likely future partners, or ideal future partners. Would they, for example, prefer a partner who is family centered? A partner who equally divides his or her commitments and responsibility between work and family? Or a partner who is career centered? If no partner comes to mind, ask that they simply consider how they now orient themselves toward their non-work and personal pursuits and examine the three possible cells they could occupy on the grid. Single people will always have both personal and family obligations that are important to them.

Small groups can be formed of those with similar patterns by putting all the "1's," "2's," "3's," and so on together or by forming small groups from various combinations of the nine cells, depending on the distribution of the large group. Then ask each small group to consider and discuss what it is like to be in a particular cell, what they see as the particular benefits and costs, and, if they have already done their career diagnoses, how it fits or does not fit with their career anchors. You might also suggest they share with one another just how they now organize their work careers and family/life activities and what difficulties they face in doing so.

As the workbook suggests, you might also ask them to predict and share where they see themselves on the grid in three or five or even ten years' time, since the cells representing particular work career/family/life patterns are often closely tied to a specific life stage of the participant. It may also be useful to ask them where they were on the grid, say, three or five years previously. This makes visible changes and possible changes in the life situations of the participants and may provide a deeper appreciation for just how they can manage their careers moving forward in a way that better meets all their life needs.

After the small group discussion, the larger group should again gather to listen and learn from report-outs by all groups on the surprises, insights, differences, and commonalities picked up in the small group sessions. It is useful to present a grid that summarizes the priorities reported by all the participants in the session. An illustration of such a grid representing a recent EMBA class at MIT in 2011 is shown in Table 4. The sixty-two students in this class were mostly U.S.-based managers between the ages of thirty-five and fifty; 80 percent reported themselves currently in a close relationships, 60 percent had children, and 35 percent were women.

Table 4. The Work/Family Priority Grid: MIT EMBA Program (2012)

		YOURSELF		
		Work Career	**Equal**	**Family/Life**
PARTNER	**Work Career**	3	6	1
PARTNER	**Equal**	15	22	1
PARTNER	**Family/Life**	8	6	0

n=62

Source: The Work Career and Family/Life Priority Grid was developed by Lotte Bailyn, MIT Sloan School of Management, 2000.

Finally, it is useful to allow for some group discussion, both with those who occupy similar positions on the grid and with those whose positions differ. This can be done in a plenary or a small group session. Conversations of this sort typically explore the various ways participants were, are, and may be challenged by particular family and personal life patterns. A good deal of learning and individual insight often result from these discussions. If participants are familiar with one another's respective career anchors, the conversation can be particularly rich. If small groups are used, asking each group to return to a plenary session with a short list of "lessons learned" is typically useful and a good way to close out the session.

Option 5: Use the Career Development Implications to Identify Personal Growth Needs

The workbook provides a fifty-item self-diagnostic checklist where the participant can rate him- or herself on Motives and Values, Analytic Abilities and Skills, Interpersonal and Group Skills, and Emotional Abilities and Skills. This can provide you and the participants a vocabulary and a set of categories that make it possible to identify where personal growth is needed if future career progress is to be achieved. The items are particularly relevant to what jobs will require in the future, given the trends that are identified in the Looking Ahead section of the workbook. This can be used with or without the career anchor materials.

Specific items as discussed in the workbook can be identified in discussions with the participant, leading up to the identification of specific developmental activities, timetables, and plans for review. Space is provided in the workbook for making such concrete plans and timetables.

How *Managers* Should Use the Survey and the Workbook

YOU MAY BE RUNNING a workshop in a company for a group of managers, or participants may want guidance on how what they have just done could be applied in their organization. *The most important point to emphasize is that if a manager decides to use these materials with his or her subordinates, he or she should complete the self-assessment and related activities first.* This is desirable because these exercises provide a good framework and vocabulary for talking about career and job issues. The most common use in organizations has been for a manager, who has seen the value of the exercise as a participant, to ask his or her subordinates to do the exercise in preparation for an annual career development session.

Most organizations require a manager to have a career development session with each subordinate once a year, preferably well separated from performance appraisal and salary review. A week or two before that session, the manager should give each subordinate copies of the self-assessment and the workbook, with the following instructions:

> "I have found the following exercise useful as preparation for a discussion of future career development. It will provide us a common vocabulary to analyze your career aspirations and what may be possible in our organization. You will not be asked to share the results of the exercise unless you choose to reveal them, but the concept of career anchors will help us to have a constructive discussion of your strengths, weaknesses, developmental needs, and future options. When we get together to discuss your development, I will ask you to share whatever you choose to, based on having done the activity."

In the actual session with each subordinate, the manager can reveal his or her own anchor to start the discussion or just talk about the process of developing self-insight vis-à-vis a career. In some organizations, managers just give out the booklet as a general career development tool, or they turn it over to their training or development staff for use in workshops and counseling.

DO NOT USE THE SURVEY AS A TEST. DO NOT USE YOUR INTUITION ABOUT SOMEONE'S CAREER ANCHOR AS A BASIS FOR JOB ASSIGNMENT. USE IT ONLY AS A GUIDE TO INCREASE YOUR SUBORDINATE'S INSIGHT INTO HIM- OR HERSELF.

How *Managers* Should Use Role Mapping in Succession Planning

MOST MANAGERS AND EMPLOYEES will agree that the rate of change in organizations is dizzying and that the management of surprise is the order of the day. Many of these changes are touched on in the Looking Ahead section of the workbook. One of the main elements of this rapidly accelerating change is that jobs themselves are becoming less clear and less bounded. If the predictions about less hierarchy and more horizontal, knowledge-based, and project-based work are at all accurate, most managerial, professional, and technical employees will find themselves switching roles frequently. Job descriptions will become increasingly obsolete because (1) they are designed to create and maintain stability, (2) they do not put enough emphasis on how jobs and roles are related to each other, and (3) they do not emphasize how jobs are changing. In their place, we will need a dynamic process that:

- Allows job holders to rapidly define and redefine their changing roles as the network around them changes to adapt to a turbulent environment;
- Allows executives and managers to figure out how roles in their organizations are changing and to communicate those changes to future job holders; and
- Provides executives and managers a powerful tool for succession planning.

Some of the trends that are creating this need are described in detail in the workbook and are summarized here:

1. Organizations worldwide are reexamining their structures and are engaging in various kinds of "downsizing," "outsourcing," "rightsizing," joint ventures, and acquisitions and mergers.
2. Globalization and new technologies have loosened the boundaries of organizations, jobs, and roles.

3. As work becomes technically more complex, fewer people will work in operational roles and more people will work in knowledge-based service and staff roles supporting the operation.
4. As conceptual work increases and job/role boundaries loosen, anxiety levels will increase.
5. In the process of changing, organizations are (1) reexamining their hierarchical structures and moving toward flatter organizations, (2) relying more on coordination mechanisms other than hierarchy, and (3) "empowering" their employees in various ways.
6. Organizations are becoming more differentiated and complex.
7. The subunits of organizations are developing subcultures that have difficulty in communicating with each other, in spite of the fact that they are increasingly interdependent.
8. Collaborative/cooperative relationships between and among subunits and subcultures are increasingly critical to organization-wide performance.
9. Organizations are becoming more dependent on lateral communication channels.
10. Socio-cultural values around family, self, and work are changing.

Who Needs Job/Role Analysis and Planning?

This kind of analysis can be applied in a wide variety of situations and for any kind of job or role by managers or by the occupants of a given job. The main categories would be

1. Any technical, professional, or managerial employee and any executive who is in an organization that is experiencing change.
2. Any manager who is involved in succession planning and/or career counseling or coaching of his or her subordinates.
3. Any employee who is uncertain or confused about his or her job responsibilities or who is entering a new assignment.

Below, we provide two examples of just where role maps were quite useful.

Example 1: The Changing Nature of Plant Management

The clearest example of the need for a role map that we have observed has been in the chemical industry, where the job of plant manager has, in some settings, undergone an almost total transformation. The job planning exercises were done with teams of plant managers both in the United States and in Europe. The typical assumption when we initially looked at the job descriptions was to treat the job primarily as a technical one and to ensure that the pool of future plant managers would be technically able to handle the increasing complexity involved. The dominant trend was perceived to be the increasing technological complexity of the manufacturing process, leading to the assumption that technical competence was the most critical future skill for plant management.

When these groups were asked to identify all of the stakeholders who have expectations of a plant manager and to analyze how those expectations may be changing in the future, a somewhat different picture emerged. First of all, the analysis revealed that the technical content of the typical plant manager's job had already become so heavy that the plant manager needed a technical staff. He or she could no longer stay on top of the technology, and key technical decisions were made primarily by the staff.

More importantly, with the advent of occupational safety concerns, societal and community environmental concerns, and growing union concerns about employment security, the plant managers found themselves increasingly negotiating with various interest groups around issues that had virtually nothing to do with the technology of the plant. The stakeholder analysis revealed that there were powerful changes occurring in the attitudes of the unions, the community, and the relevant government agencies that had little to do with technological niceties of the production process, except where they specifically impacted safety, quality of work life, or the environment.

In each relationship with a stakeholder, what the plant manager was perceived to be doing more and more was negotiating in a complex political environment. As a result of this insight, the company realized that what it needed in its future plant managers was not technocrats but very talented negotiators who were willing and able to spend time working on the plant's various external interfaces. Internal relations and technical matters were increasingly handled by the manager's staff and subordinates.

The job had been changing for a number of years, but this had not been explicitly observed or analyzed; hence little provision was made in the human resource planning and development processes to identify and develop such future negotiators. Individual plant managers experienced a sudden insight into the causes of their frustrations in that they realized that they felt unprepared to do things that were outside of their formal job descriptions. As a result of these insights, the company immediately instituted a different system of appraising performance and potential in the manufacturing management area and started up new development programs to ensure that its vision of what the job of the future would be could be fulfilled.

Plant managers who participated in the exercise had a sense of relief that what they were increasingly experiencing was valid, not simply an indication that they were doing a bad job or concentrating on the wrong things. They were able to clarify in their own minds the importance of managing the external interfaces and, more importantly, now found it legitimate to ask for training and advice in these more "soft" and political areas.

Example 2: Spontaneous Redesign of a Job/Role

The power of using a role map for succession purposes was illustrated in a company that had recently lost its vice president for administration. When the members of the executive committee met to work on who should replace the lost executive, it was apparent that they had one candidate in mind, Joe, but they also had some reservations about him. They discussed all the pros and cons of giving Joe the job, citing his strengths and weaknesses in general personality terms and in terms of his past job history: he was a good manager, but not so good in his external relations; he handled people well; he knew the technical areas of the company well; and so on. On the whole, the picture was very positive, but somehow the group could not agree that he was right for the job.

At this point, questions about the job itself were raised: What exactly did the vice president for administration do? Who are the major stakeholders surrounding that job? How did they see the job changing in the future? In answer, the group started to list areas like personnel, legal, purchasing, information systems, and public relations. When they came to this last item, someone interrupted and said, "You know, as I think about it, Joe is good in all of those areas except public relations. He is just not good with outsiders and, as we look ahead, those outsider relationships are going to become much more important."

This comment produced immediate agreement from the whole group and led one member to a big insight. He asked the group whether public relations had to be part of this job. After only a few moments, the group agreed that public relations did not have to be part of the job of vice president of administration. In fact, the other parts of the job were growing so rapidly that there was already enough in the job, and the tasks related to public relations could easily be shifted to one of the other senior vice presidents until a permanent person could be found to do solely public relations. Once they had redesigned the job, they quickly reached complete consensus on Joe's appropriateness for it and, incidentally, discovered that public relations was going to become so important in the future that they needed a full-time person to do it.

These examples illustrate the importance for the key executives who are doing succession planning to think more systematically about the ways a specific job or cluster of organizational jobs is changing. Building a role map provides a systematic way to do so. We often assume that the present structure of jobs is appropriate and only reexamine individual jobs when major reorganizations occur. But restructuring of the sort that the two examples illustrate should become more and more common as the environment becomes more dynamic and stakeholder expectations change.

Succession Planning Exercise

How role maps can be determined and used by managers is rather straightforward. For each of the jobs that managers have to fill and for which they are required to have "people in the pipeline" and, most importantly, for their own jobs, they should get together with some colleagues who are subordinates, some who are peers in related jobs, and some who are at a higher level and do the following steps:

Step 1: For a given job, gather three or four people who are currently part of the role set of that job for a one-hour meeting.

Step 2: Draw a complete role map for that job. (See Step 1: Create a Role Map in The Role Map: Analyzing Your Present Situation section of the workbook, page 55 to 58.)

Step 3: Identify key stakeholders and determine whether their expectations will be likely to change in the next five years based on technological, economic, and socio-cultural trends.

Step 4: List the implications of the changes you have identified for the competencies that will be needed in that job as you look ahead. Chances are that these are not identified in the current job description.

Step 5: Gain group consensus on what the key requirements will be for the job as you look ahead and incorporate those into the current job description. Redesign the job if it appears appropriate based on what you have learned.

Step 6: Share the revised job description and the role map with applicants for the job. If you and they have taken the *Career Anchors Self-Assessment,* discuss how well matched the job and the career anchor are. Create a climate of openness that allows each of you to identify mismatches.

Workshop Designs and Topics

THESE MATERIALS CAN BE used in many different ways with a wide variety of participants. We suggest here a few variations that have worked consistently well but would encourage facilitators to design their own workshops to suit their particular situations. We will review what can be done in half a day or less. If you have more time, you can easily adapt what we suggest by lengthening each step.

Half-Day Career Anchor Workshop

(See also Option 2 in the How to Use the Participant Workbook section.)

Participants: 5 to 50

Goals

- To help each participant to develop self-insight so that he or she can manage career choices and moves
- To offer participants a set of concepts and a framework for thinking about how careers develop and fit into total lifestyles
- To provide participants an opportunity to practice interviewing and being interviewed about career development, something that is especially useful if participants are managers who have to do career coaching of their own subordinates

Materials

- A copy of the *Career Anchors Self-Assessment* survey and the *Participant Workbook* for each participant
- Flip charts

- Markers
- Masking tape

Physical Setting

The room should contain movable chairs so that participants can easily pair up for the mutual interview portion; alternatively, the setting has to have spaces for participants to go off and do their interviews.

Procedure and Timing

- **Introduction and overview (10 to 15 minutes).** Give a brief review of the concept of Career Anchors and what is in the self-assessment and workbook, but give out only the self-assessment at this time. The actual eight anchors should NOT be revealed or reviewed at this time to avoid premature bias. The goals of the workshop should be reviewed.
- **Ask participants to fill in the self-assessment (15 minutes).** Whether or not participants should do the scoring at this point is up to you. However, the different speeds at which people work and their own curiosity make it almost impossible to keep participants from transferring their numbers, adding up the scores, and looking at the descriptions of the anchor categories.
- **Hand out the workbook and ask participants to pair up and do the mutual interviews (150 minutes).** Refer the participants to the pages in the workbook that give the instructions and questions for the interview. Tell participants not to read other parts of the workbook at this time to avoid bias.

  To help participants with the pairing up, point out that it is best to work with someone who knows them well, whether or not they are in the same organization. The exception to this suggestion is when participants can do this interview with a spouse who may be attending the workshop. For obvious reasons, however, in the workshop setting, try to avoid linking up a boss and subordinate as a pair. In some workshops, the participants come from different countries and may have language problems. In that case, encourage people to work with partners who speak the same language.

Point out that the important information to be gathered is what the person did and what the reasons were for doing it. Tell interviewers to listen for the pattern of responses in the reasons why things were done. Ask people to return to the plenary session in 150 minutes promptly to facilitate total group discussion. Point out as people prepare to leave that it is fun to talk about your own career and, therefore, to monitor the time so that both participants in the pair have that chance.

Suggest the following timing for the pairs:

- A interviews B for about one hour
- A and B look at B's survey scores and discuss what B's anchor is for 15 minutes
- B interviews A for about one hour
- B and A look at A's survey scores and discuss what A's anchor is for 15 minutes

- **When they return, lead a total group discussion (30 minutes)**. Ask the group how it felt to be interviewed and to do an interview; draw out some of the positive aspects of reflecting on one's own career and listening to someone else's career adventures.

  Encourage questions about the process of identifying one's anchor. These questions almost always deal with several specific issues that are reviewed below.

  If there is time and if the group seems relaxed, put the anchor categories on a flip chart and ask how many people chose each category as their first or second choice. That produces the insight that there is almost always a lot of variation in the anchors, even though the participants may all be from one occupation or organization. If there is a bias toward some anchors, ask the group to speculate with you what the implications are. Especially encourage the group to discuss whether the culture they are in makes some anchors more desirable than others and ask whether they think that biased their responses.

  Discuss the implications the career anchor diagnosis may have had for them in the time remaining, drawing on the points listed below.

  Encourage participants to read the rest of the workbook and to do the various diagnostic tasks on their own.

Answers to Frequently Asked Questions and Learning Points to Be Emphasized in the Total Group Session

Question: Can I have more than one anchor?

Early in our careers, we value a great many things and, therefore, do not yet know what we would hold on to if forced to make a choice. The further into a career we are, the more likely it is that there will be just one anchor.

Question: Is my anchor what I am actually doing or what I would like to be doing?

Many people are in jobs that do not feel right in terms of their anchors, so the anchor in those cases is what you would like to be doing. People are in such jobs for many reasons, such as family circumstances, a tight labor market, health constraints, early bad decisions, and so on. Many people don't "find themselves" until later in their careers, but their anchors have been active in guiding them toward what they eventually "really wanted to do." Where jobs and anchors are mismatched, one often finds people expressing their anchors in hobbies or second jobs.

Question: Are some anchors better/more desirable than others?

In some cultures, there are biases toward some anchors. For example, in the United States we tend to glorify the managerial, entrepreneurial, and challenge anchors and to look down on people who are security anchored. In Australia, it turned out to be just the opposite in a number of workshops because it is not appropriate to appear too self-centered in that culture, so people who had the managerial anchors tended to deny it in public. In any case, the important thing is to know what one's anchor is, quite apart from whether or not one makes it public. In terms of some absolute standard, every anchor is equivalently valuable.

Question: Do anchors change?

Change is certainly possible and cases can be found, but the odds are against it for several reasons. As we gain self-insight, this provides security and direction, so the more we know about ourselves as we age, the more stable we become and the more stable we want to remain. When we encounter people who seem to have made major career changes later in life and ask them about it, it often turns out that they were "finally doing what they had always wanted to do," but never had the chance or the means to do it earlier in their careers. In other words, the anchor did not change, but it took a long time for the person to do what his or her anchor demanded.

The cases that have been followed up in research suggest strongly that, once the person knows his or her anchor, the person tends to organize his or her career and life to maintain it, not change it. Change in anchors probably only occurs if the person has had some powerful life-changing experience that brings out new facets of his or her personality.

Question: How do I define "success" in my career?

How the culture defines success in the external career and how the person defines success in his or her internal career can be quite different. Internally, success is defined by achieving what one's career anchor demands—using one's talents, meeting one's needs, and operating consistently with one's values. That will differ in each anchor group; hence there is no one criterion of success. For example, money or rank is primarily a measure of success in the managerial anchor group, whereas professional reputation among peers is primarily a measure of success in the technical/functional anchor group.

Question: Is the anchor concept valid in other cultures?

The anchor concept is definitely valid and useful in all the Western/English-speaking cultures. These booklets have been translated into Japanese and Chinese as well as Spanish and Portuguese for use in South America. As we said above, cultures vary in how they view careers and the "desirable" anchor may vary culture by culture, but the concept that people are in their careers for different reasons and must learn to manage their own careers appears to be increasingly true everywhere.

Final Learning Points

Highlight the following information:

- Different people, even in the same occupation, have different career anchors.
- What people with different anchors seek is quite different, which is especially exemplified by the fact that not everyone is "managerial" in the sense of wanting to climb the corporate ladder and make lots of money.
- Knowing what one is good at, wants, and values is essential to making good career and life choices in the future.
- It is important to communicate one's self-insight to one's boss and others in organizations that have power over one's career development.

Two-Hour Career Anchor Workshop

This shorter design has the same goals as the half-day design, requires the same set-up, and should be introduced in the same way. Time can be saved by shortening the introduction and debriefing session and by asking the participant pairs to do only one career history interview during the workshop, deferring the other one for some time on their own. This is not ideal and often not workable, but since the workbook and self-assessment are designed to be self-administering, it is possible to ask the participants to do some of the work on their own. One variation of this would be to ask people to do the interviews with their partners or close friends prior to coming to the workshop—as suggested by Option 2 earlier—and using the time in the workshop to explore in some detail the anchors themselves and the implications. This variation is similar to what can be done with classes in which the interviews are required homework between two class sessions that are some days or weeks apart.

Use of Role Mapping and the Work Career and Family/Life Grid

In all of the workshop settings it is desirable to allow time for these two additional exercises following the work on career anchors. There are no specific rules for how much time so facilitators should make their own judgments on the overall workshop organization. But we have found that the ideal career and life planning workshop includes all the elements—self-assessment, mutual interviews, role mapping, and work/life analysis. These components give the participant a complete picture of what he or she needs to think about in terms of future personal development and growth.

Development Planning

WHEN THE PARTICIPANTS HAVE finished their anchor analysis, role map analysis, and work career and family/life exercises, you may want to help them to formulate development plans for themselves. Instead of using vague general terms for development, the last section of the workbook, Implications for Your Career Development, provides a list of all the specific competencies, motives, and values that have been identified in relation to those career anchors that are organizationally relevant. They are associated especially with the general managerial anchor.

Participants can assess themselves on all fifty items and identify those that pertain especially to what their anchor analyses have told them are the important characteristics of their career anchors. The workbook is self-explanatory, but in a workshop context it may be useful to discuss how to use the items developmentally.

Implications and Conclusions

SUCCESSFUL ORGANIZATIONAL PERFORMANCE AND PRODUCTIVE, SATISFYING CAREERS are ultimately the product of a good process of matching the ever-changing needs of organizations with the ever-changing needs of individual career occupants. All indications are that the rate of change is increasing, so this matching problem will be more acute than ever in the future.

The individual career occupant has a responsibility to know what he or she wants and requires out of a career and any given job. Such self-insight comes from experience and from systematic self-diagnosis. We should all know what our career anchors are so that we can make better choices and negotiate better with organizations when we are confronted with job opportunities and options. But what of the organization's responsibility?

We would argue that organizations have not done a good job of understanding the work to be done to meet organizational needs; and even when they do understand the work to be done, they have not done a good job of communicating what those needs and expectations are. The primary purpose of role mapping is to improve that process of planning and diagnosing work and then communicating the diagnosis to job incumbents. In other words, individuals cannot really do their jobs and make good career choices if the information available about the work and career options is incomplete, superficial, or inaccurate.

The organization is an abstraction, but the individual employee or manager is not. We would argue that all employees and managers, as part of their basic jobs, must have a complete understanding of their own work and the work to be done under them and around them. And they must have the skill to communicate that understanding to the subordinates, peers, and superiors who must carry out the work. Inasmuch as the work is perpetually changing, employees and their managers must perpetually think about and plan for all the jobs that they are responsible for or connected with. This exercise is designed to facilitate such planning and is, therefore, an integral tool in the process of fulfilling both individual and organizational needs.

Career development for the individual and better job placement for the organization can only be achieved if individuals do a better job of figuring out and communicating their own career anchors and if organizations do a better job of analyzing jobs in terms of role requirements and communicate those more clearly to the job applicants. You, as facilitator, have a role to play in making clear to your participants that they can influence their own organizations to be more responsible in analyzing work and communicating what it really entails.

References and Additional Reading

Acemoglu, D., & Autor, D.H. (2011). Skills, tasks and technologies: Implications for employment and earnings. *Handbook of Labor Economics, 4*, 10043–1171.

Arthur, M.B., Inkson, K., & Pringle, J.K. (1999). *The new careers*. Thousand Oaks, CA: Sage.

Arthur, M.B., & Rousseau, D.M. (Eds.). (1996). *The boundaryless career*. New York: Oxford.

Autor, D.H., Katz, L.F., & Kearney, M.S. (2008). Trends in U.S. wage inequality: Revising the revisionists. *The Review of Economics and Statistics, 90*(2), 300–323.

Bailyn, L. (1978). Accommodation of work to family. In R. Rapoport & R.N. Rapoport (Eds.), *Working couples*. New York: Harper & Row.

Bailyn, L. (1992). Changing the conditions of work: Implications for career development. In D.H. Montross & C.J. Schinkman (Eds.), *Career development in the 1990s: Theory and practice*. Springfield, IL: Thomas.

Bailyn, L. (2002). *Beyond work-family balance: Advancing gender equity and workplace performance*. San Francisco: Jossey-Bass.

Bailyn, L. (2011). *Breaking the mold: Redesigning work for productive and satisfying lives* (2nd ed.). Ithaca, NY: Cornell University Press.

Barley, S.R., & Kunda, G. (2006). *Gurus, hired guns, and warm bodies: Itinerant experts in the knowledge economy*. Princeton, NJ: Princeton University Press.

Barth, T.J. (1993). Career anchor theory. *Review of Public Personnel Administration, 13*, 27–42.

Benko, C., & Weisberg, A. (2007). *Mass career customization*. Boston: Harvard Business School Press.

Bianchi, S.M., Casper, L.M., & King, R.B. (Eds.). (2005). *Work, family, health, and well-being*. Mahwah, NJ: Lawrence Erlbaum Associates.

Briscoe, J.P., & Hall, D.T. (2006). The interplay of boundaryless and protean career attitudes: Combinations and implications. *Journal of Vocational Behavior, 69*, 4–18.

Briscoe, J.P., Hall, D.T., & Mayrhofer, W. (2011). *Careers around the world: Individual and contextual perspectives.* London: Routledge.

Crepeau, R.G., Crook, C.W., Goslar, M.D., & McMurtney, M.E. (1992). Career anchors of information systems personnel. *Journal of Management Information Systems, 9*, 145–160.

Davis, S.M., & Davidson, B. (1991). *2020 vision.* New York: Simon and Schuster.

Derr, C.B. (1986). *Managing the new careerists.* San Francisco: Jossey-Bass.

Durcan, J., & Oates, D. (1996). *Career paths for the 21st century.* London: Century Business Press.

Edmundson, A.C. (2012). *Teaming: How organizations learn, innovate, and compete in the knowledge economy.* San Francisco: Jossey-Bass.

Farber, H.S. (2010). Job loss and the decline in job security in the United States. In K. Abraham, J. Spletzer, & M. Harper (Eds.), *Labor in the new economy.* Chicago: University of Chicago Press.

Fine, C. (1999). *Clockspeed: Winning industry control in the age of temporary advantage.* New York: Basic Books.

Gittell, J.H. (2009). *High performance healthcare: Using the power of relationships to achieve high performance.* New York: McGraw-Hill.

Goffman, E. (1963). *Stigma.* New York: Simon and Schuster.

Gunz, H., & Peiperl, M. (Eds.). (2007). *Handbook of career studies.* Thousand Oaks, CA: Sage.

Hall, D.T. (2002). *Careers in and out of organization.* Thousand Oaks, CA: Sage.

Harrington, B., & Hall, D.T. (2007). *Career management and work-life integration: Using self-assessment to navigate contemporary careers.* Thousand Oaks, CA: Sage.

Harrison, B. (1997). *Lean and mean: Why large corporations will continue to dominate the global economy.* New York: Guilford Press.

Higgins, M.C. (2005) *Career imprints.* San Francisco: Jossey-Bass.

Ho, K. (2009). *Liquidated: An ethnography of Wall Street.* Durham, NC: Duke University Press.

Hochschild, A.R. (1997). *The time bind: When work becomes home and home becomes work.* New York: Holt.

Hochschild, A.R. (2012). *The outsourced self: Intimate life in market times.* New York: Metropolitan Books.

Ibarra, H. (2003). *Working identity: Unconventional strategies for reinventing your career.* Boston: Harvard Business School Press.

Jacobs, J., & Gerson, K. (2004). *The time divide: Work, family and gender inequality.* Cambridge, MA: Harvard University Press.

Kellogg, K. (2011). *Challenging operations: Medical reform and resistance in hospitals.* Chicago: University of Chicago Press.

Khurana, R. (2002). *Searching for the corporate savior: The irrational quest for charismatic CEOs.* Princeton, NJ: Princeton University Press.

Klinenberg, E. (2012). *Going solo: The extraordinary rise and surprising appeal of living alone.* New York: Penguin.

Kochan, T.A. (2010). *Resolving America's human capital paradox: A proposal for a jobs compact.* Paper posted on the website of the Employment Policy Research Network. Available: www.employmentpolicy.org.

Kossek, E., & Lambert, S. (Eds.). (2005). *Work and life integration: Cultural and individual perspectives.* Mahwah, NJ: Lawrence Erlbaum Associates.

Malone, T.W. (2004). *The future of work: How the new order of business will shape your organization, your management style, and your life.* Boston: Harvard Business School Press.

Mishel, L., Bermstein, J., & Shierhotz, H. (2009). *The state of working America, 2008–2009.* Ithaca, NY: Cornell University Press.

Newman, K.S. (2012). *The accordion family: Boomerang kids, anxious parents, and the private toll of global competition.* Boston: Beacon Press.

Nordvik, H. (1991). Work activity and career goals in Holland's and Schein's theories of vocational personalities and career anchors. *Journal of Vocational Behavior, 38,* 165–178.

Nordvik, H. (1996). Relationships between Holland's vocational typology, Schein's career anchors, and Myers-Briggs' types. *Journal of Occupational and Organizational Psychology, 69,* 263–275.

Osterman, P. (2009). *The truth about middle managers: Who they are, how they work, how they matter.* Boston: Harvard Business School Press.

Percheski, C. (2008, June). Opting out? Cohort differences in professional women's employment rates from 1960 to 2005. *American Sociological Review, 73*(3), 497–517.

Perlow, L.A. (2012). *Sleeping with your smartphone: How to break the 24/7 habit and change the way you work.* Boston: Harvard Business School Press.

Poelmans, S.A.Y. (Ed.). (2005). *Work and family: An international research perspective.* Mahwah, NJ: Lawrence Erlbaum Associates.

Reitman, F., & Schneer, J.A. (2003). The promised path: A longitudinal study of managerial career. *Journal of Managerial Psychology, 18,* 60–75.

Savitz, A.W., & Weber, K. (2006). *The triple bottom line: How today's best-run companies are achieving economic, social, and environmental success.* San Francisco: Jossey-Bass.

Schein, E.H. (1971). The individual, the organization, and the career: A conceptual scheme. *Journal of Applied Behavioral Science, 7,* 401–426.

Schein, E.H. (1975). How career anchors hold executives to their career paths. *Personnel, 52,* 11–24.

Schein, E.H. (1977). Career anchors and career paths: A panel study of management school graduates. In J. Van Maanen (Ed.), *Organizational careers: Some new perspectives.* Hoboken, NJ: John Wiley & Sons.

Schein, E.H. (1978). *Career dynamics: Matching individual and organizational needs.* Reading, MA: Addison-Wesley.

Schein, E.H. (1987). Individuals and careers. In J. Lorsch (Ed.), *Handbook of organizational behavior.* Englewood Cliffs, NJ: Prentice-Hall.

Schein, E.H. (1996). Career anchors revisited: Implications for career development in the 21st century. *Academy of Management Executive, 10,* 80–88.

Schein, E.H. (2010). *Organizational culture and leadership* (4th ed.). San Francisco: Jossey-Bass.

Sennett, R. (2006). *The culture of the new capitalism.* New Haven, CT: Yale University Press.

Turco, C. (2012). Difficult decoupling: Employee resistance to the commercialization of personal settings. *American Sociological Review, 118*(2), 380—419.

U.S. Census Bureau. (2010). *Married couple family groups by labor force status of both spouses.* Washington, DC: Author. Available: www.bls.gov/population/socdemo/hh-fam.

Van Maanen, J., & Schein, E.H. (1977). Career development. In J.R. Hackman & J.L. Suttle (Eds.), *Improving life at work.* Santa Monica, CA: Goodyear Publishing.

Yarnall, J. (1998). Career anchors: Results of an organization study in the UK. *Career Development International, 3,* 55–61.

About the Authors

Edgar H. Schein was educated at the University of Chicago; at Stanford University, where he received a master's degree in psychology; and at Harvard University, where he received his Ph.D. in social psychology in 1952. He is Sloan Fellows Professor of Management Emeritus at MIT's Sloan School of Management. Previously, he was chief of the Social Psychology Section of the Walter Reed Army Institute of Research while serving in the U.S. Army as Captain from 1952 to 1956. He joined MIT's Sloan School of Management in 1956 and was made a professor of organizational psychology and management in 1964. From 1968 to 1971, Dr. Schein was the undergraduate planning professor for MIT, and in 1972 he became the chairman of the Organization Studies Group of the MIT Sloan School, a position he held until 1982. He was honored in 1978 when he was named the Sloan Fellows Professor of Management, a Chair he held until 1990.

Dr. Schein has been a prolific researcher, writer, teacher, and consultant. Besides his numerous articles in professional journals, he has authored fourteen books, including *Organizational Psychology* (3rd ed., 1980), *Career Dynamics* (1978), *Organizational Culture and Leadership* (1985, 1992, 2010), *Process Consultation Vol. 1 and Vol. 2* (1969, 1987, 1988), *Process Consultation Revisited* (1999), and *The Corporate Culture Survival Guide* (2009). Dr. Schein wrote a cultural analysis of the Singapore Economic Development Board entitled *Strategic Pragmatism* (MIT Press, 1996) and has published an extended case analysis of the rise and fall of Digital Equipment Corporation entitled *DEC Is Dead; Long Live DEC: The Lasting Legacy of Digital Equipment Corporation* (Berrett-Koehler, 2003). He was co-editor with the late Richard Beckhard of the Addison-Wesley Series on Organization Development, which has published over thirty titles since its inception in 1969. He has consulted extensively on career development and corporate culture in the United States and abroad.

Dr. Schein received the Lifetime Achievement Award in Workplace Learning and Performance from the American Society of Training Directors (2000), the

Everett Cherington Hughes Award for Career Scholarship from the Careers Division of the Academy of Management (2000), the Marion Gislason Award for Leadership in Executive Development from the BU School of Management Executive Development Roundtable (2002), the Lifetime Achievement Award as Scholar/Practitioner from the Academy of Management (2009), and the Lifetime Achievement Award from the International Leadership Association (2012).

John Van Maanen works within the fields of organization behavior and theory. He is an ethnographer of organizations ranging in type from police organizations to educational institutions as well as a variety of business firms. He has taught in the Sloan School of Management at MIT since 1972. In 1988 he was named the Erwin Schell Professor, a Chair he still holds. He has been a visiting professor at Yale University, University of Surrey, and INSEAD in France. His undergraduate education was at the California State University at Long Beach, and he earned his Ph.D. from the University of California at Irvine.

Dr. Van Maanen has published a number of works in the general area of occupational and organizational sociology. Cultural descriptions figure prominently in his studies of the work worlds of patrol officers on city streets in the United States, police detectives and their guv'nors in London, fishermen in the North Atlantic, MBA students at MIT and Harvard Business School, and park operatives in the Sistine Chapel of Fakery, Disneyland (here and abroad). He is the author and editor of numerous books, including *Organizational Careers* (1977), *Policing: A View from the Street* (1978), *Tales of the Field* (University of Chicago Press, 2nd ed., 2011), *Qualitative Studies of Organizations* (1999), and *Organizational Transformations and Information Technology* (with Joanne Yates, 2001).

Dr. Van Maanen is a member of the American Sociological Association and a Fellow of the American Association of Applied Anthropology. He has served on the editorial boards of a variety of journals, including *Administrative Science Quarterly, Human Organizations, Journal of Contemporary Ethnography, Human Relations,* and, most recently, *Journal of Organizational Ethnography*. He has worked with numerous public and private organizations in North America, Europe, and Asia, including, recently, Li and Fung, BP, Moller-Maersk, U.S. Internal Revenue Service, Lafarge, Warburg Dillon Read, and Hong Kong University. He was the faculty chair of the Sloan Fellows Program at MIT from 1994 to 2000 and the faculty chair of the Organization Studies Group (1995 to 2000, 2003 to 2008).

CPSIA information can be obtained
at www.ICGtesting.com
Printed in the USA
BVHW091532191219
567002BV00006B/101/P

9 781118 455746